# LEVERS

ANGELA ROYSTON

Heinemann
LIBRARY

**www.heinemann.co.uk.**
Visit our website to find out more information about Heinemann Library books

To order:
☎ Phone ++44 (0)1865 888066
🗎 Send a fax to ++44 (0)1865 314091
🖥 Visit the Heinemann Bookshop at www.heinemann.co.uk to browse our catalogue and order online.

First published in Great Britain by Heinemann Library,
Halley Court, Jordan Hill, Oxford OX2 8EJ,
a division of Reed Educational and Professional Publishing Ltd.
Heinemann is a registered trademark of Reed Educational & Professional Publishing Limited.

OXFORD MELBOURNE AUCKLAND
JOHANNESBURG BLANTYRE GABORONE
IBADAN PORTSMOUTH NH (USA) CHICAGO

Designed by Visual Image
Illustrations by Barry Atkinson
Originated by Dot Gradations
Printed in Hong Kong/China

04 03 02 01 00
10 9 8 7 6 5 4 3 2 1

ISBN 0431 01742 5

British Library Cataloguing in Publication Data

Royston, Angela
Levers. - (How it works)
1.Levers - Juvenile literature
I.Title
621.8'11

Acknowledgements

The Publishers would like to thank the following for permission to reproduce photographs: Cumulus: Trevor Clifford pp8, 15, 18, 22, 23; Garden and Wildlife Matters: p10; Heinemann: Trevor Clifford pp4, 7, 11, 14, 17, 20, 21, 23, 24, 28, 29; Impact: Piers Cavendish p5; Pictor Uniphoto: p25; Robert Harding Picture Library: p16; Telegraph Colour Library: Space Frontiers Ltd p27; Tony Stone Images: Don Spiro p12, Joe Cornish p19; Travel Ink: Tony Page p9

Cover photograph reproduced with permission of Milepost 92½.

The Publishers would like to thank Anthony Mirams for his help and advice with the text and Jo Brooker for making the models on p28-9.

Every effort has been made to contact copyright holders of any material reproduced in this book. Any omissions will be rectified in subsequent printings if notice is given to the Publisher.

Any words appearing in the text in bold, **like this**, are explained in the Glossary.

# CONTENTS

# What do levers do?

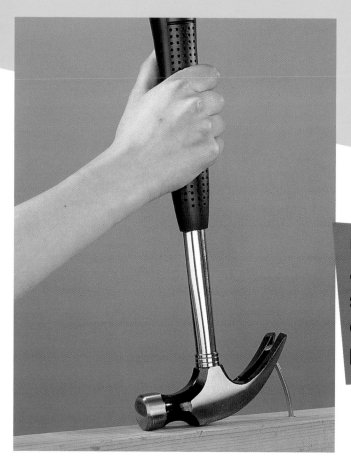

Using a hammer as a lever, only a small amount of effort is needed to pull the nail out.

How can you make yourself stronger than you are? The answer is by using a **machine**. Some machines are complicated and use a motor or engine to give them power. A few machines are so simple you might not think of them as 'machines'. Levers, wheels, screws, springs, ramps and pulleys are simple machines that have been used for thousands of years.

This book is about levers. A lever is a long, thin rod or stick that makes things move. It is often used to lift weights up, to balance weights and to cut things.

**4**

# Think about it!

Look at the picture of the roadworks below. The wheelbarrow and the spade are two levers which you can find out about in this book.

**Builders use many kinds of lever to help them lift things and move things.**

## Lifting the world

A lever is extraordinarily powerful. With a simple lever you could lift an enormous elephant. Archimedes was a Greek who lived nearly 2300 years ago. He worked out the scientific law that governs how levers work and said, 'Give me a place to stand and I will move the Earth.'

# How a lever works

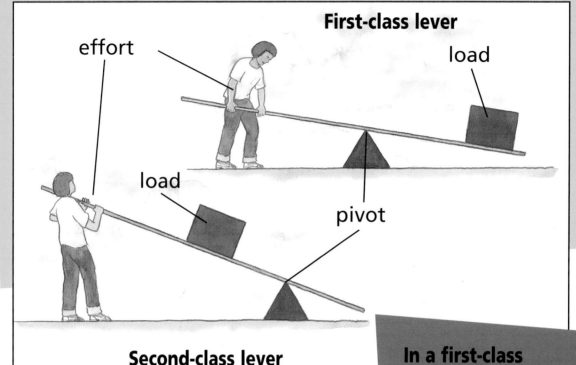

**First-class lever**

effort

load

load

pivot

**Second-class lever**

To move something, you have to push it or pull it. The **force** used in the push or pull is called the **effort**. The thing you want to move is called the **load**.

In a first-class lever, the pivot is between the effort and the load. In a second-class lever, the load is between the pivot and the effort.

## The pivot

A lever works by turning around a point, called the **pivot**. In the pictures above, the pivot is the block of wood that supports the lever. As the effort moves one end of the lever down, the end on the other side of the pivot moves up. If the pivot was not there, the whole lever and load would fall to the ground. The load is easiest to lift when the effort is as far as possible from the pivot and the load is close to the pivot.

# Try this!

You will need one thick book (the load), a wooden block (the pivot), and three strong rulers – a short one, a medium one and a very long one. Put each ruler in turn over the pivot and place the book on one end. Push the other end of the ruler down. Which ruler needs the least effort to lift the book? Which lever needs most effort?

This person is using a lever to lift a heavy metal cover. He puts the lever under the edge then pushes down. The load is much closer to the pivot than the effort is. This makes it easier to lift.

pivot

effort

load

# Stronger than you think

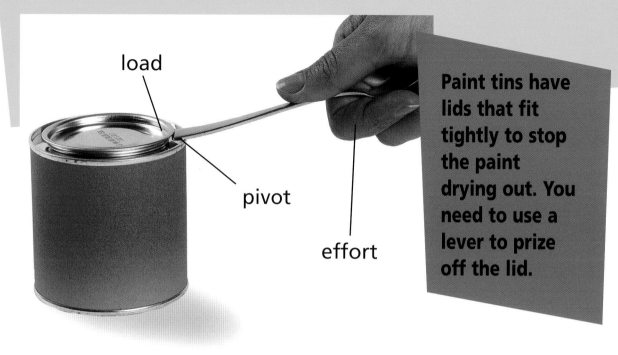

load

pivot

effort

Paint tins have lids that fit tightly to stop the paint drying out. You need to use a lever to prize off the lid.

A lever changes a small **force** into a big one. It would be very difficult to get a lid off a tin, using just your fingers. But if you put the end of a spoon underneath the lid and push down gently you can lift the lid up.

## Less effort

A long spoon makes lifting even easier because it spreads out the effort of lifting. Your hand moves down a long distance to lift the **load** (the lid) a short way. The farther away the effort is from the **pivot**, the less effort is needed.

A wheelbarrow makes lifting easier because you lift the handles farther than you lift the load. The wheelbarrow in the photo is a **second-class lever**. The load is between the pivot and the effort.

# Think about it!

The longer a lever, the easier it is to lift the load. So why does a wheelbarrow not have handles which are two metres long? What would happen then? Why does a wheelbarrow have only one wheel? What would be the advantages and disadvantages of having two, three or four wheels?

A wheelbarrow is a lever. When the barrow is full, the gardener lifts the handles to move the load. The barrow's pivot is the centre of the wheel. The wheel helps the barrow move forward easily.

load

effort

pivot

# Changing pull to push

Digging earth is hard work, but using a fork as a lever makes it easier. What kind of lever is the fork?

It is easier to push down than to pull up. A lever changes pull to push. A garden fork, for example, makes it possible to lift up by pushing down. You push the fork into the earth and then push the handle down (the **effort**) to lift up the earth (the **load**). It is not always easy to see where the **pivot** is. Here the pivot is where the fork rests against the ground. What other garden tools are used as levers?

# Make it work!

You may like to climb trees, but it is often hard to reach the first branch. Draw a design for a lever to help you lift your friend up high. It will need a pivot, a handle and a special end to carry your friend. What shape will you use for the carrier?

**The tip of the bottle-opener pivots on the cap to lift up the rim.**

push down

pull up

## Bottle-opener

The bottle-opener is a **second-class lever**. The pivot is the tip of the opener which rests on the cap. The claw catches on the cap (the load) and prizes it up.

# Oars and paddles

In a rowing boat, the rower leans back to pull the boat forward through the water. The rowlock stops the oar slipping along the boat. What else does it do?

Levers can help you move more easily and quickly through the water. A rowing boat has two levers (the oars) which pivot at the **rowlocks**. Is the oar a **first-class lever** or a **second-class lever**?

Sometimes everything in boats seems to be back to front. The rower faces backwards in order to go forwards. In an oar, the **effort** is closer to the **pivot** than the **load** (the water). It would take less effort if it was the other way round. But what would happen then? In rowing, you lean back a short way, to pull the load a long way through the water.

load

effort

pivot

## Canoes

A paddle is a lever too. But it is neither a first-class nor second-class lever. As the canoeist pulls the paddle through the water it pivots around the upper hand. In this case, the effort (the lower hand) is between the pivot and the load (the part of the paddle in the water). A paddle is an example of a **third-class lever**.

The paddle is a third-class lever. The effort (the hand) moves a short way to make the load move a long way.

## Think about it!

Suppose you found a boat but it had no oars or paddles. The only things you could use as a paddle were a broom, a frying pan, a spade or a tennis racket. Which would make the best paddle? What other things would make a good paddle?

# Balancing act

Levers can be used to make things balance. In a balance scales the rod that joins the two **pans** is a lever. It **pivots** in the centre so that each pan is the same distance from the pivot. The scales balance when the **effort** (the weights) equals the **load** (the object being weighed).

To find out how much something weighs, add weights to one pan until they balance the object in the other pan.

14

**The woman is heavier than the child. What can they do to balance the seesaw?**

# The seesaw

The seesaw is also a lever that pivots in the centre. If two children who are about the same weight sit at each end, the seesaw will be balanced. If one child sits closer to the pivot, their effort (weight) will have less effect and the seesaw will go up at that end. If one child is heavier than the other, the seesaw will go down at their end.

Seesaws in parks and playgrounds usually use **springs** to help to keep the seesaw balanced. This means the children do not have to be exactly the same weight to balance the seesaw.

## Try this!

Make a seesaw using a ruler and a triangular block for the pivot. Put other small blocks on each side of the seesaw. How many ways can you get two blocks to balance one block?

# Tower crane

The crane driver lowers the hook at the end of the long cable to pick up a heavy load.

The tower crane uses the laws of levers to balance its **load**. The **boom** of the tower crane **pivots** around the driver's cab. Can you see the big block on the short end of the boom, behind the driver? The block is called a **counter-weight** because it balances the weight of the load.

The counter-weight is nearer to the pivot than the load and so it has to be much heavier than the load. When the crane picks up a very heavy load, the driver moves the hook closer to the cab to balance the load.

# Think about it!

Suppose that the crane driver puts down a heavy load of metal beams and then picks up a lighter load of window frames. Which way should he move the hook – towards the cab or away from it?

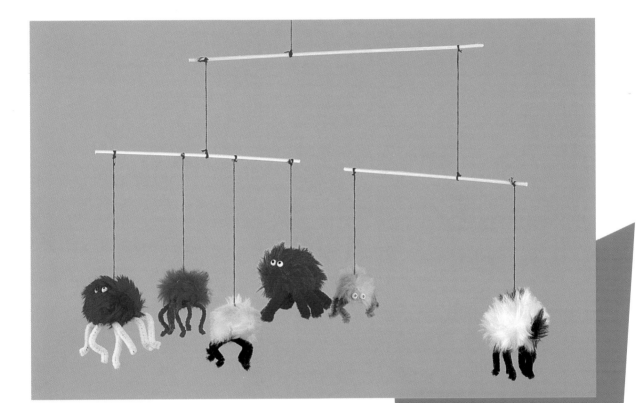

# A mobile

Look at the top rod of the mobile. Four shapes are hanging from one end and only two are hanging from the other end. The top rod is balanced because the pivot (the thread it is hanging from) is closer to the heavier end.

**Each rod of the mobile hangs by a thread tied to the rod above. Each rod acts as a lever that pivots around the knot of the thread.**

# Bridges

When a boat or ship is taller than a bridge, the bridge must be lifted to let the boat through. The bridge across the canal is attached to a lever. When the handle of the lever is pulled down, the other end lifts up one side of the bridge. The person pulling the lever is helped by a heavy weight on the end of the lever handle. The weight balances the weight of the bridge. The person only has to add a small amount of **effort** to lift the bridge.

**Using a lever and a counter-weight, one person can lift the bridge all on their own.**

Tower Bridge in London is in two halves. When a tall ship needs to pass through it, the traffic is cleared and each half swings up.

# Tower Bridge

Each side of Tower Bridge weighs about 1000 tonnes, as much as 5000 strong men! Heavy weights on the outer end of each side balance the weight. **Electric motors** are used to lift the bridge. But the **counter-weights** are so accurate the motors are no bigger than the motor used in a lawn mower.

## Try this!

Make a model to show how Tower Bridge works. Use short rulers for the two parts of the bridge. Place each on a support such as a wooden block and position them so that they just touch. Use modelling clay to balance the weight of the rulers. Can you make your bridge strong enough to take a small model car?

# Scissors and wire-cutters

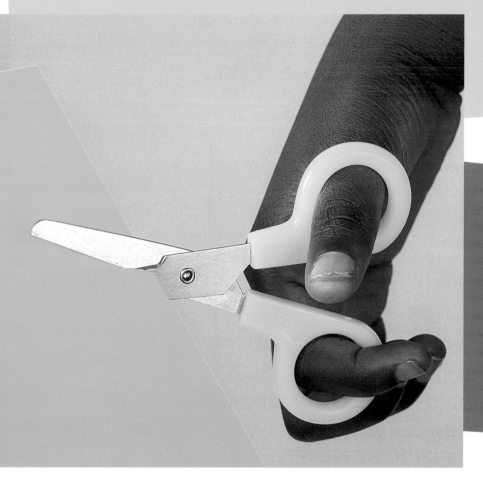

**Scissors are a double lever. Squeezing the handles together gives a strong force between the blades.**

A pair of scissors is useful for cutting paper, cloth, plasters and other things. They may not look like levers, but they are. In fact, they are not just one lever, but two levers working together. The **pivot** is in the middle, so each lever is a **first-class lever**.

As you squeeze the handles together (the **effort**), the blades are pushed together to cut the paper. The scissors have short handles and long blades. This makes it easier to control the amount the scissors cut. Always be careful not to cut yourself when you use scissors.

This engineer is using a pair of wire-cutters. The cutters are so powerful they can cut through thick wire and even metal rods.

# Wire-cutters

The wire-cutters have long handles and short blades. The effort which the **engineer** applies to the handles is much further from the pivot than the wire he is cutting (the **load**). He only has to use a small effort to get a strong **force** between the blades.

# Pliers and nutcrackers

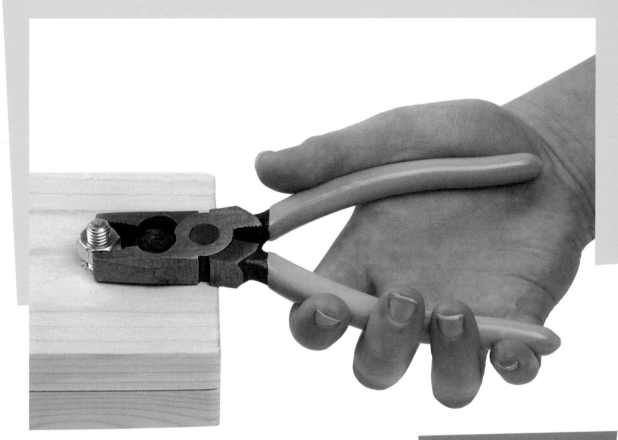

Pliers are double levers that are used to grip things tightly. When you squeeze the handles, it produces a strong squeezing **force** between the jaws. The jaws have many grooves. These help the pliers to grip without slipping.

Pliers are useful for unscrewing a tight nut. The pliers grip the nut tightly and the handles provide a long lever.

The pliers are designed so that the jaws always grip the nut squarely. This is different from a pair of scissors, where the blades meet at a 'V'.

## Think about it!

Tweezers are double levers too. What kind of double levers are they?

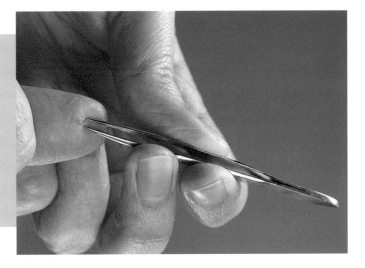

# Nutcrackers

Nutcrackers are **second-class double levers**. The **load** is between the handles and the **pivot** is at the end. Nutcrackers are shaped to hold a small nut or a large nut, such as a walnut. When you squeeze the handles, the nutcrackers magnify your **effort**. The handles are levers that pivot about the end and squeeze the walnut until it cracks.

The walnut splits open under the pressure from the nutcracker.

# Levers that push levers

To stop a bike, you pull the brake lever on the handle bars. Follow the wire to the levers that push the brake blocks against the wheel.

In some **machines**, several levers work together. Sometimes the levers are linked by wires or **cables**.

There are two brake levers on the handle-bars of a bicycle. One works the brakes on the back wheel and the other the brakes on the front wheel. Each brake lever is joined to metal **calipers** by a strong wire. When you pull the brake lever, the wire pulls the metal calipers on each side of the wheel. The calipers push the **brake blocks** against the rim of the wheel and so make the wheel slow down.

**24**

## Did you know?

An **excavator** uses **hydraulic power** to move its levers. Hydraulic power works by forcing oil through a narrow tube. It is another way of turning a small **force** into a large one. To see how this works, squeeze the end of a hose-pipe while water is running through it. The water shoots out more powerfully when the end is small.

In an excavator three main levers work together to guide the bucket.

boom   dipper

## Excavators

The excavator arm is in three parts – the **boom**, the dipper and the bucket. The boom raises and lowers the dipper. The dipper **pivots** where it joins the boom. It moves the bucket backwards and forwards. The bucket tilts up and down to dig and to empty.

# Piano keys

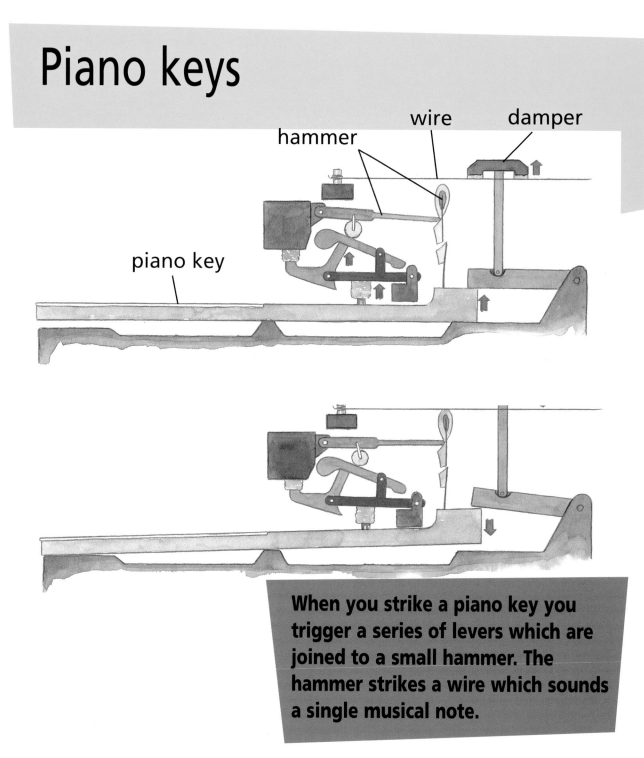

hammer

wire

damper

piano key

**When you strike a piano key you trigger a series of levers which are joined to a small hammer. The hammer strikes a wire which sounds a single musical note.**

Each key on a grand piano is joined to a hammer which strikes a particular note. The sound is made by the **vibrations** of a tight wire. After the note is struck a **damper** moves down to stop the wire vibrating. If it didn't, the note would go on sounding, as it does when you hold the key down.

# Striking a note

A small movement on the key lifts the red lever. This lifts the orange lever and the hammer. The hammer strikes the wire above. The levers change the small movement of the key to a large movement of the hammer. At the same time the green lever at the end of the piano key lifts the damper off the wire to let it vibrate.

When you take your finger off the piano key, the hammer moves smoothly down. The damper drops back onto the wire to stop the note sounding. The pianist can play the notes quickly and clearly because the system works so smoothly.

## Think about it!

The Space Shuttle's robot arm is a series of levers. It is used to move satellites in or out of the spacecraft's loading bay. Only a small **effort** is needed to work the arm in space. Why do you think that is so?

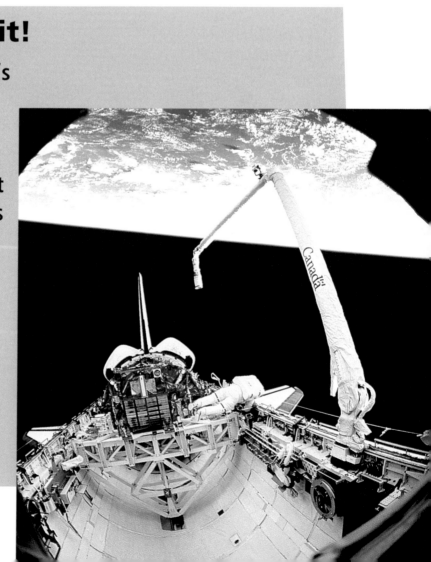

# Make a pop-up card

A hidden lever pushes the clown's legs and arms up and down.

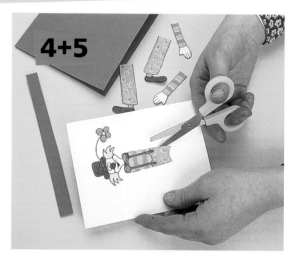
4+5

## You will need:

- a large piece of thick paper or thin card
- 2 paper fasteners
- coloured pens, pencil, scissors, glue

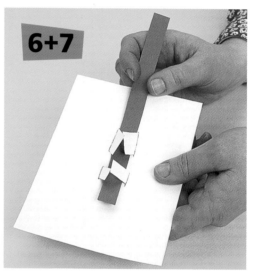
6+7

1, 2+3

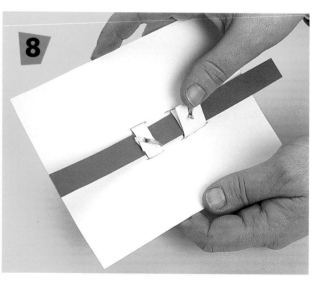
8

1 Cut a piece of card 30 cm by 20 cm. Fold it down the middle to give a card 15 cm wide and 20 cm deep.

2 Cut another piece of card 13 cm wide by 18 cm deep. On it draw the head and body of a clown and pencil in the legs and arms.

3 On a spare piece of paper, draw the legs and arms. Make them longer than you want them to appear on the finished card.

4 Cut a slider 2 cm wide and 20 cm deep.

5 Colour in all the parts of the clown. Cut vertical slots in the body of the clown where the arms and legs should go.

6 Push the arms and legs through the slots and turn them to point down. Turn the clown over.

7 Place the slider over the back of the clown so that 1 cm shows above and below the paper. Mark where the arms and legs meet the slider. Trim them if they are too long.

8 Make a hole through the slider and the arms and push a paper fastener through. Make another hole through the slider and the top of the legs and push the other paper fastener through.

9 Put glue around the edge of the paper, but not where the slider crosses it.

10 Carefully glue the clown inside the card.

11 When the glue is dry, pull the slider to see the clown's arms and legs lift up.

# Glossary

**boom** long arm of a crane or excavator to which a hook or bucket is attached

**brake block** rubber block that rubs against a bicycle wheel to slow it down

**cable** a thick wire

**caliper** metal arm

**counter-weight** a weight that balances a load

**damper** a lever which stops the note made by a piano key

**effort** the force applied to a lever to move the load

**electric motor** an engine that uses electricity to move something

**engineer** someone who designs or works with machines, bridges, transport and other technical things

**excavator** machine used for moving earth

**first-class lever** a lever in which the pivot is between the effort and the load

**force** a push or pull that makes something move

**hydraulic power** force produced by liquid being squashed in a thin tube

**leverage** ability to act as a lever

**load** the weight or force that a lever moves or balances

**machine** a device that allows you to do something more easily or that you couldn't do on your own

**pans** a set of scales has two pans, one to hold the weights and the other to hold the load

**pivot** the point on a lever round which the lever turns

**rowlock** a metal peg which supports and holds the oar in a rowing boat

**second-class lever** a lever in which the load is between the pivot and the effort

**springs** something which returns to its original shape after being stretched or squashed

**third-class lever** a lever in which the effort is between the load and the pivot

**vibrations** small, fast movements backwards and forwards

# Answers to questions

**p7** The longest ruler should lift the books more easily. The shortest ruler should need the most **effort**.

**p9** Very long handles would make it awkward to push the wheelbarrow around corners and difficult to tip up to empty. Three or four wheels would mean that you did not have to lift the wheelbarrow to push it, but the wheels would be more likely to get stuck in wet mud and loose ground.

**p10** A fork is a **first-class lever**. A spade, trowel and hoe are levers too.

**p12** An oar is a first-class lever.

**p12** Photo: The **rowlock** supports the oar and acts as the **pivot**.

**p12** If the rowlock were closer to the water than the rower's hand, each stroke would take very little effort, but the end of the oar in the water would not move very far. So the boat would not move very far either.

**p13** A spade has a long handle and a flat end so it would make the best paddle because it would push more water on each stroke.

**p15** The woman should move closer to the pivot in the middle of the seesaw.

**p17** When the driver picks up a lighter **load** he should move the hook away from the cab. He can also move the counter-weight closer to the cab.

**p21** The part of the blades nearest the pivot cut best, because the effort is strongest there.

**p23** Tweezers are **third-class double levers**. The effort is between the pivot and the load.

**p27** Satellites are weightless in space so Space Shuttle's robot arm works on very little power.

# Index

## Titles in the *How it Works* series include:

Hardback    0 431 01742 5

Hardback    0 431 01744 1

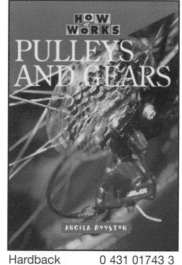

Hardback    0 431 01743 3

Hardback    0 431 01745 X

Hardback    0 431 01747 6

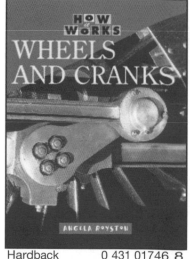

Hardback    0 431 01746 8

Find out about the other titles in this series on our website www.heinemann.co.uk/library

# Answers to questions

**p7**   The longest ruler should lift the books more easily. The shortest ruler should need the most **effort**.

**p9**   Very long handles would make it awkward to push the wheelbarrow around corners and difficult to tip up to empty. Three or four wheels would mean that you did not have to lift the wheelbarrow to push it, but the wheels would be more likely to get stuck in wet mud and loose ground.

**p10**  A fork is a **first-class lever**. A spade, trowel and hoe are levers too.

**p12**  An oar is a first-class lever.

**p12**  Photo: The **rowlock** supports the oar and acts as the **pivot**.

**p12**  If the rowlock were closer to the water than the rower's hand, each stroke would take very little effort, but the end of the oar in the water would not move very far. So the boat would not move very far either.

**p13**  A spade has a long handle and a flat end so it would make the best paddle because it would push more water on each stroke.

**p15**  The woman should move closer to the pivot in the middle of the seesaw.

**p17**  When the driver picks up a lighter **load** he should move the hook away from the cab. He can also move the counter-weight closer to the cab.

**p21**  The part of the blades nearest the pivot cut best, because the effort is strongest there.

**p23**  Tweezers are **third-class double levers**. The effort is between the pivot and the load.

**p27**  Satellites are weightless in space so Space Shuttle's robot arm works on very little power.

# Index

# Titles in the *How it Works* series include:

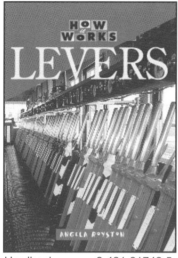

Hardback       0 431 01742 5

Hardback       0 431 01744 1

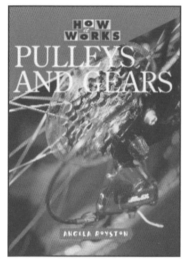

Hardback       0 431 01743 3

Hardback       0 431 01745 X

Hardback       0 431 01747 6

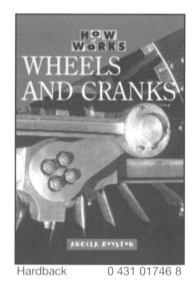

Hardback       0 431 01746 8

Find out about the other titles in this series on our website www.heinemann.co.uk/library